DISCOVER

CATHEDF FROM ABOVE

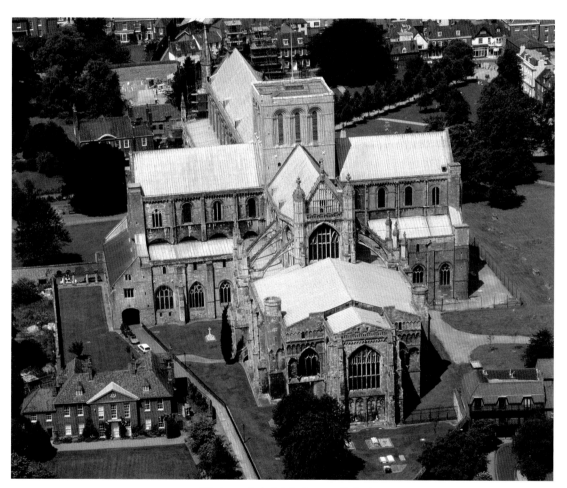

Winchester Cathedral, the longest in England

JOHN MANNION

MYRIAD
LONDON

WESTMINSTER ABBEY *left*

ALL BUT TWO OF ENGLAND'S MONARCHS SINCE 1066 have been crowned at Westminster Abbey. As a "royal peculiar" the abbey is not attached to any diocese and has been at the centre of the nation's political life since it was founded by Edward the Confessor. The original building was in the Norman-French style but it was almost wholly rebuilt in the new Gothic style starting in the reign of Henry III. The high roof and narrow nave are based on French models whereas the long nave and broad transepts are typically English. Work initiated by Henry continued for a further 250 years.

Meanwhile pilgrimages to the shrine of St Edward the Confessor and royal patronage made the Abbey immensely wealthy. It was the repository of important royal documents and the King's council often took place in the Chapter House. The Treasury was held in the Chapel of the Pyx until at least the 15th century and Westminster also housed the Exchequer. The Abbey suffered badly during the Reformation but the building as it is today was completed in 1745 to the designs of Wren and Hawksmoor.

WESTMINSTER CATHEDRAL *below*

ALTHOUGH WESTMINSTER CATHEDRAL was built on land formerly owned by a pre-Reformation Benedictine community it actually replaced Tothill Fields Prison. The Diocese of Westminster was created in 1850 at the Restoration of the Catholic hierarchy but it had to wait a further 44 years before work could begin on its new cathedral. Work was completed on the building in 1903.

Designed by John Francis Bentley the cathedral is a neo-Byzantine basilica based on early Christian Mediterranean churches and inspired by buildings such as Hagia Sophia in Istanbul, San Vitale in Ravenna and St Mark's in Venice.

The exterior consists of finely detailed brickwork alternating with bands of Portland stone while the interior is intended to be covered in Byzantine-style mosaics. Only a small proportion of the mosaics are in place even today but the colour and brightness of the interior is enhanced by over 125 varieties of marble. Entrance to the cathedral is via an open piazza which also contains a *campanile*.

St Paul's *left*

ST PAUL'S CATHEDRAL, BUILT BETWEEN 1675 and 1710 and designed by Sir Christopher Wren, is the fourth cathedral to occupy the site. The previous one was destroyed in the Great Fire of London. It is the largest cathedral in England and was the first church in England to incorporate a dome. Elsewhere Wren included a wide range of classical and neo-classical features based on the very best of contemporary European architectural techniques.

The exterior of the building has changed little since 1710 but the interior has been frequently modified. Highlights include Tijou's wrought iron gates, the mid 19th-century mosaics and the organ that was once played by Mendelssohn. The crypt contains effigies and fragments of stone from earlier incarnations of the cathedral and the famous Whispering Gallery allows people to hear each other from either side of the dome.

The cathedral has witnessed the funerals of Lord Nelson, the Duke of Wellington and Sir Winston Churchill as well as the wedding of Prince Charles to Lady Diana Spencer.

Southwark *above*

SOUTHWARK CATHEDRAL WAS BUILT ON THE site of a Roman villa and some of its pavements are still preserved in its floor. Construction of St Mary Overie (over the river) was begun in 1106. A fire in 1212 led to a major rebuilding in the Gothic style. Southwark Cathedral is now one of the oldest Gothic buildings in London.

After the Reformation St Mary Overie became the parish church of St Saviour. In Mary Tudor's reign an ecclesiastical court was set up in the retro-choir and seven men were condemned to death there for heresy. Later the retro-choir fell into disrepair and was rented out as a bakery; other parts of the building were used as a pottery and a starch factory. Under James I, St Saviour was the parish church of what was then London's theatre and entertainment district. Names of many actors from Shakespeare's time appear in the church's registers.

The church declined considerably until the late 19th century when, after it survived a campaign to knock it down, a new nave was constructed and other restoration work began. The church became a cathedral in 1905.

CANTERBURY *above*

THE CATHEDRAL AT CANTERBURY began its history when St Augustine arrived there as a missionary in 597AD. The present building, which has evolved since the Norman period, is a mixture of Gothic and perpendicular styles.

The Cathedral is most famous for its many distinguished archbishops (there have been 104 of them) including St Augustine, St Dunstan, St Anselm and St Thomas à Beckett. Thomas was a friend of King Henry II when he was appointed to the see of Canterbury and was expected to support the monarchy above the Church. In fact he did the opposite and was murdered in his cathedral on 29 December 1170 by four officious knights who were responding to Henry's question: "Who will rid me of this turbulent priest?" The Archbishop was declared a martyr and shortly after his canonisation pilgrimages to his tomb began. These were immensely popular in the middle ages and continue today.

ROCHESTER *right*

FOUNDED IN 604 ROCHESTER IS THE second oldest cathedral in England. Earlier buildings were replaced by Bishop Gundulf, William the Conqueror's chief castle builder, and the squat Norman parts of the cathedral are still in evidence. Later building programmes introduced the Romanesque, Gothic and Early English elements. The Norman nave contrasts strongly with the Gothic arches of the crossing and there is a richly carved stone archway of the Decorated period (c1345) that leads into the chapter room. Other interesting features include an unusually sited Lady Chapel; a very well-preserved vaulted crypt; and some fragments of medieval ceiling paintings. Rochester was a popular centre for pilgrimage during the 13th century.

The cathedral shares a dramatic location on the banks of the Medway with the 13th-century Rochester Castle, once besieged for over two months by King John in 1215.

ST ALBANS *above*

SAINT ALBANS CATHEDRAL IS BELIEVED to be built on the site of the execution of Britain's first Christian martyr, St Alban, in 250AD. The present abbey church was begun in 1077 and used bricks from the ruins of the nearby Roman city of Verulamium. The 11th-century bell tower is the only remaining example of its type, and the nave is the longest in England. The nave features both rounded Norman arches and pillars and decorated style columns dating from 1323.

Among the cathedral's treasures are a series of 13th and 14th-century wall paintings and the 14th-century shrine of St Alban. In 1539 the Benedictine Abbey of St Albans was dissolved and the church served its local parish until the creation of the diocese of St Albans in 1877 when it became a cathedral. In 1862 extensive restoration work was undertaken by Sir George Gilbert Scott.

Christ Church, Oxford *above*

CHRIST CHURCH CATHEDRAL is the smallest cathedral in England and also functions as a college chapel. Parts of the present building date back to the 12th century but most are the result of Cardinal Wolsey's project to found Cardinal College in 1522. The west end was demolished and a highly elaborate replacement planned, but the Cardinal fell out of favour with Henry VIII in 1529 and the improvements never took place. The king took over the chapel to be the cathedral church of the newly created diocese of Oxford in 1546. The bell tower at the front of the college was designed by Sir Christopher Wren to house the great Tom bell. Cathedral services still run on Tom time which is five minutes behind Greenwich Mean Time.

Scenes in the *Harry Potter* films were shot in Christ Church College, thus continuing an association with children's literature that goes back to the 19th century. *Alice's Adventures in Wonderland* was written by college fellow Lewis Carroll.

✳

Guildford *left*

GUILDFORD CATHEDRAL IS ONE OF the few Church of England cathedrals to be newly built since the Reformation. It was begun in 1936 to a design by Sir Edward Maufe, and dedicated in 1961. Standing on a hill above the town of Guildford, the cathedral dominates its surroundings and is floodlit at night. The interior is spacious with honey-coloured stone walls and marble flooring. On the top of the cathedral is an unusual golden archangel weathervane.

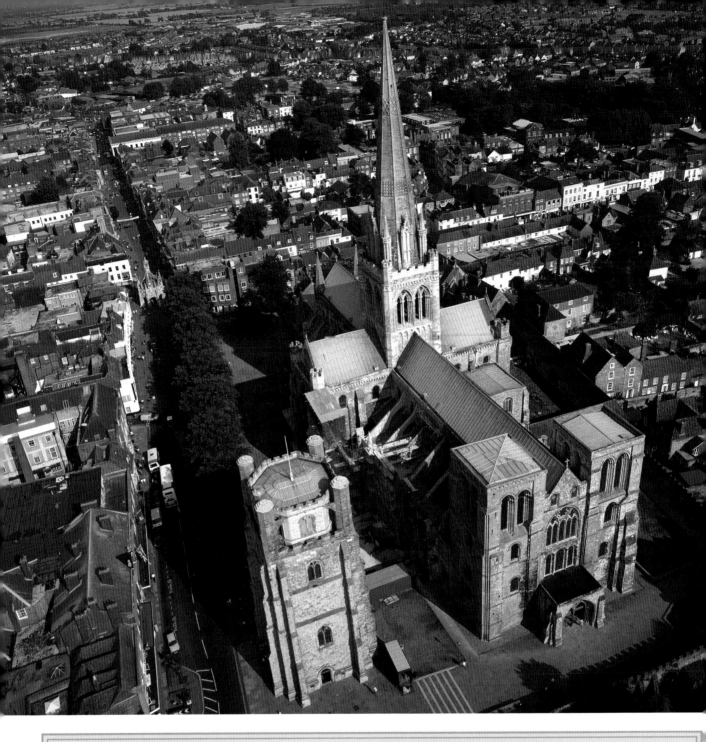

CHICHESTER *above*

THE SEE OF CHICHESTER WAS FOUNDED in 1076 and its cathedral was completed in 1108. Major renovations took place in 1187, following a fire, when much of the present stonework and flying buttresses were constructed. In the 13th century Bishop Richard of Chichester was canonised and the cathedral became a centre for pilgrimages in his honour. A shrine was built for him in the retro-choir and at about the same time the Lady Chapel was extended and fitted with windows in the decorated style. In the 15th century a spire was added along with a detached bell tower; the only one of its kind now remaining in England.

The cathedral was badly damaged during the Reformation and Civil War periods. The shrine of St Richard was destroyed; brasses were removed; stone figures and carvings were defaced and the medieval stained-glass was smashed. Restoration began in the 1840s but the spire collapsed in 1861 and had to be completely replaced.

WINCHESTER *right*

DURING THE ANGLO-SAXON PERIOD THE church on the site of Winchester Cathedral was dedicated to St Swithun. Given that saint's connection with rain it is not surprising that Winchester cathedral is much troubled by water. Even today the vaulted Norman crypt is subject to flooding; at the beginning of the 20th century a diver, William Walker, had to spend up to six hours a day in 20 feet of water and total darkness for six years in order to restore the 11th-century timber rafts.

The cathedral, which is the longest in England, was begun in the Norman period but it has been re-modelled and rebuilt on several occasions. The cathedral houses the shrine of St Swithun as well as the graves of King Alfred the Great and Jane Austen together with a statuette commemorating the "Winchester diver". Although it suffered some destruction after the Dissolution of the Monasteries, Winchester has been skilfully restored both internally and externally.

BATH *above*

BATH ABBEY IS THE THIRD GREAT CHURCH to stand on its site in the last twelve and a half centuries. An Anglo-Saxon abbey church, begun in 757, was replaced by a Norman cathedral from about 1090 which was in turn replaced by the present church which dates from 1499. The Norman church fell into ruin because it was too expensive for its supporting abbey to run and the present church was ruined after the dissolution of the monasteries. It was subsequently restored by the local community.

Dating as it does from 1499, Bath Abbey is one of the last great medieval churches of England. Its unique west front depicts the dream of its founder, Bishop Oliver King, that prompted him to raise the present building over the Norman ruins. An early 16th-century fan-vaulted ceiling is one of the most impressive aspects of the interior.

BRISTOL (ST MARY REDCLIFFE) *right*

QUEEN ELIZABETH I WAS GREATLY taken with St Mary Redcliffe – so much so that, in around 1574, she proclaimed it:

"The fairest, goodliest and most famous parish church in England."

Parts of St Mary Redcliffe date back to the 12th century, though most of the current building was completed in the 15th century and restored during the Victorian era. It is a fine example of Gothic architecture. The outer north porch, built around 1280, is an unusual octagonal shape and protects an earlier more sacred porch. The spire, completed in 1872, is 292ft (89m) high. The church and its history are thought to have inspired the work of the poet Thomas Chatterton and, as a result of this association, it received many visits from Romantic poets including Coleridge, Wordsworth and Shelley.

WELLS *left*

THE FIRST OF MANY CHURCHES AT WELLS was built in the early 8th century; and the first cathedral dates from the middle of the 10th century. However in 1088 Wells lost its cathedral status and did not regain it until 1245. Construction of the present building began in 1180 and continued for the next 300 years.

Wells is one of Britain's smaller cathedrals but it is also one of its most beautiful. The 13th-century west front is 100ft (30.5m) high and 150ft (45.75m) wide (twice the width of the nave) and contains niches for more than 500 figurative sculptures, most of them larger than lifesize. Almost 300 of the statues are original medieval works of art.

The nave contains a unique "scissor-arch", which supports the weight of the central tower, as well as a Saxon font and a 14th-century painted clock. The beautifully vaulted, octagonal Chapter House still contains fragments of medieval glass as well as some amusing carved corbels between the stalls. The polygonal Lady Chapel has a spectacularly painted roof vault.

✳

EXETER *below*

THE SEE OF EXETER WAS ESTABLISHED by Edward the Confessor in 1050 but work on the cathedral did not start until the Norman period in 1114. The two Norman towers have survived from the original building but the majority of the cathedral is in decorated Gothic-style. Building started in 1270 and continued for over a hundred years. As many as 20 chantry chapels were also added in the medieval period. During the Reformation the cathedral was cleansed of many of its statues and paintings but the decorated bosses and corbels survived and only one statue was lost from the Image Screen.

In the Civil War the cathedral was divided between Presbyterians and Congregationalists. A wall was built across the choir screen; the Presbyterians occupied the choir and the Congregationalists worshipped in the nave. The choir was restored by Gilbert Scott in 1870. In 1942 the cathedral suffered a direct hit during a bombing raid but, despite severe damage, no major structural problems were caused and the damage has since been restored.

TRURO *right*

THE BISHOPRIC OF CORNWALL WAS re-founded in 1876 and a new cathedral was begun in Truro in 1880. The first part of the cathedral was consecrated in 1887 and the whole building was completed by 1910. Designed by John Loughborough Pearson, Truro was the first British cathedral to be consecrated after the Reformation.

The cathedral grew out of St Mary's Church which dates back to 1259. One aisle of the old church remained, and from it the rest of the neo-Gothic cathedral emerged.

Pearson's intention was to induce awe in the minds of visitors and he used size and scale to do so. Influenced by churches in Normandy and Brittany which "grow" out of their local communities, Truro rises above the local shops and offices.

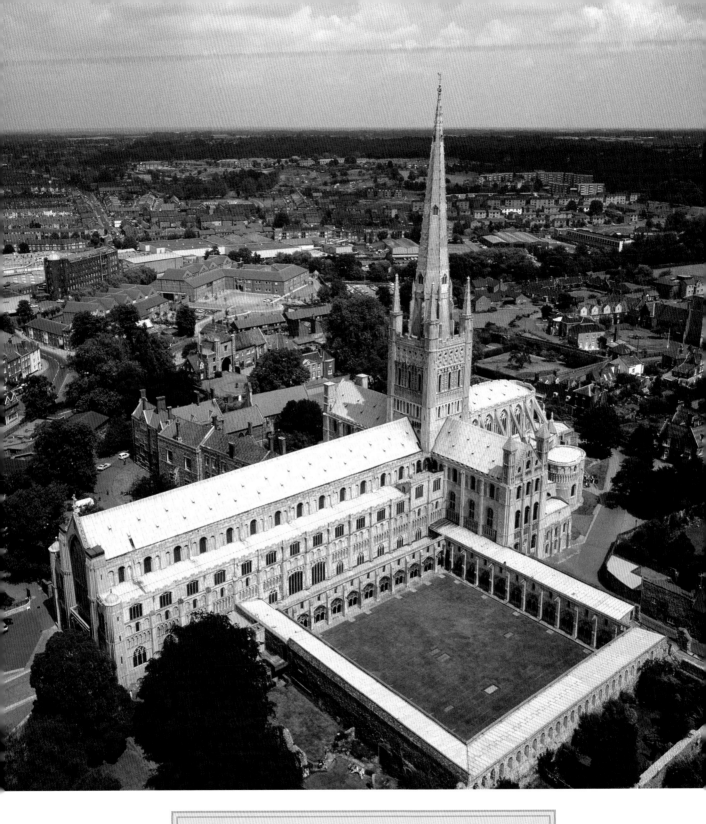

NORWICH *above*

FOUNDED IN 1096 NORWICH CATHEDRAL is one of the finest complete Romanesque buildings in Europe and has the second highest spire in England. The nave roof is set with over 1,000 carved bosses that depict Biblical characters and scenes; incidents from the lives of the saints; scenes of everyday life; and images of the Green Man. The aisle is unusually long and has 14 bays.

The spire has been struck by lightning twice, once in 1463 when a disastrous fire ensued and once in 1999 when a lightning conductor prevented further damage. The building has also been damaged by other fires, post-Reformation vandalism and riots by the people of Norwich.

LINCOLN CATHEDRAL WAS CONSECRATED in 1092 but was extensively damaged by an earthquake in 1185. The cathedral was rebuilt in Gothic style with flying buttresses being used to support higher walls with larger windows. The central tower collapsed in 1237 and was eventually replaced by a higher tower with a spire. In fact all three towers have had spires at some time in the history of the building but all have been removed for structural reasons.

A highlight of the cathedral is the massive west front. This has remained in place as the rest of the building extended eastwards. It was extensively damaged during the Civil War and many of its unique carvings are still being replaced or restored.

SOUTHWELL MINSTER *left*

SOUTHWELL MINSTER WAS FOUNDED IN 1108 and substantially completed by about 1150. An Early English Gothic choir screen was added in 1234 and the Chapter House, said to be one of the finest in an English cathedral, was created in 1286. A decorated style choir screen was built in 1350 with few other major changes since.

The Minster survived the Reformation relatively unscathed but was severely damaged during the Civil War. Horses are said to have been stabled there and Scottish troops vandalised the Archbishop's Palace. In 1711 the south-west spire was struck by lightning and the nave caught fire. Repairs were completed by 1720 but the nave and transepts were given flat panelled ceilings.

Restoration by Ewan Christian in the mid 19th century gave the west towers their unique and distinctive "pepperpot" spires. The flat panelling was removed from the nave and a new roof fitted. The Minster became a cathedral in 1884 when the Diocese of Southwell (north-east of Nottingham) was formed.

PETERBOROUGH *below*

THERE HAS BEEN AN ABBEY AT Peterborough since 655 but the present cathedral dates from 1118 and was consecrated in 1238. Generally it is in the Romanesque style except for the Gothic Western transept and West Front. Some further buildings were added at the beginning of the 16th century but the structure of the building is essentially as it was 800 years ago.

The West Front, with its three arches, makes a dramatic entrance to a building which contains Romanesque columns, Saxon carvings, a unique painted nave ceiling and elaborate 16th-century fan vaulting.

The abbey became a cathedral at the time of the Reformation and contains the graves of two queens: Catherine of Aragon and Mary Queen of Scots. Mary's grave is now empty as she was re-buried in Westminster in 1612. During the Civil War the cathedral lost all of its stained-glass and many of its monuments and memorials and the central tower had to be rebuilt in the 1880s. In 2001, a fire broke out and the cathedral suffered smoke damage, requiring extensive renovation.

COVENTRY *left*

COVENTRY'S EARLIEST CATHEDRAL was founded in 1043. This grew throughout the middle ages and its size and splendour were a testament to the wealth and prosperity of Coventry at that time. On the dissolution of the monasteries the See of Coventry and Lichfield was transferred to Lichfield and the former cathedral fell into disrepair. However, in 1918 a new See of Coventry was created and St Michael's became its cathedral.

On 14 November 1940 the city of Coventry was devastated by a heavy German bombing raid and several incendiary devices destroyed most of the medieval cathedral. The decision to rebuild was taken almost immediately but the new cathedral was not completed until 1962. The design was by Sir Basil Spence and the new building contains notable examples of modern art such as Sutherland's tapestry of *Christ in Glory*, Epstein's *St Michael and the Devil* and Hutton's *Saints and Angels* screen.

HEREFORD *left*

CHRISTIAN WORSHIP HAS TAKEN PLACE on the site of Hereford Cathedral for over 1,300 years. The earliest surviving parts of the building date from the Norman period and can be seen in the simplicity of the south transept and the massive round pillars of the nave. Romanesque capitals decorate the area behind the high altar and the Lady Chapel is one of the earliest and best examples of Gothic architecture in England. Substantial work on the cathedral was completed by the late 14th century.

The cathedral was damaged during the Reformation and the Civil War and fell into decay; this led, in 1786, to the collapse of the entire west end. James Wyatt was commissioned to restore the damage but most of his Gothic work was replaced in 1908. Two of Britain's most important historical treasures, the *Mappa Mundi* and the Chained Library, are housed in the award-winning New Library Building at the west end of the cathedral.

LICHFIELD *below*

THE FIRST CHURCH ON THIS SITE was built to honour St Chad in about 700 and the present cathedral still contains his shrine. A Norman cathedral was begun in the late 11th century. The choir dates from 1200 while the nave was started in 1260. Other notable additions to the building were a unique *pedilavium* where feet were washed on Maundy Thursday and an octagonal Chapter House. The Chapter House now holds the cathedral's most valued treasure, an 8th-century illuminated manuscript known as the Lichfield Gospels. Fierce fighting including three sieges took place in Lichfield during the Civil War and the cathedral was heavily damaged. Restoration was slow and it was not until the end of the 18th century that James Wyatt undertook major structural work. Wyatt's alterations were ill-conceived and 60 years later Sir George Gilbert Scott began the process of returning the cathedral to its medieval glory.

LIVERPOOL (ANGLICAN) *below*

THE ANGLICAN SEE OF LIVERPOOL was created in 1880 and its first bishop was installed in Saint Peter's Church, which was later described as "ugly and hideous". A decision to build a new cathedral was taken in 1901 and, following a design competition won by Sir Giles Gilbert Scott, the foundation stone was laid in 1904. The first part of the cathedral to be completed was the Lady Chapel in 1910 and the cathedral was consecrated in 1924. Work continued on the building even during the Second World War. The city of Liverpool was heavily bombed but the cathedral was left largely untouched. Sir Giles Gilbert Scott placed the final stone at the top of the 331ft (101m) tower in February 1942. The cathedral was officially completed in 1978.

Liverpool is the largest cathedral in Britain and the fifth largest in the world. It houses the largest church organ in the UK, built by the Liverpool firm of Henry Willis from 1923-6.

LIVERPOOL (CATHOLIC) *right*

FROM THE TIME OF THE REFORMATION until 1850 Catholics were forbidden to worship in public. As soon as the Catholic hierarchy was restored and the diocese of Liverpool created, plans began to be made for a cathedral to serve Liverpool's large Catholic population. The first attempt, designed by Edward Pugin, was started in 1853 but never fully completed.

In 1933 the foundation stone was laid for a new cathedral on the site of a former workhouse. Designed by Sir Edwin Lutyens the building was to have been a colossal domed structure rising to a height of 520ft (159m). Only the crypt was completed before the project became too expensive. An attempt was made to scale down the building but eventually a new design was chosen by competition. Sir Frederick Gibberd's design for the Cathedral of Christ the King is an expression of the new liturgical spirit fostered by the Second Vatican Council. It was completed within five years and consecrated in 1967.

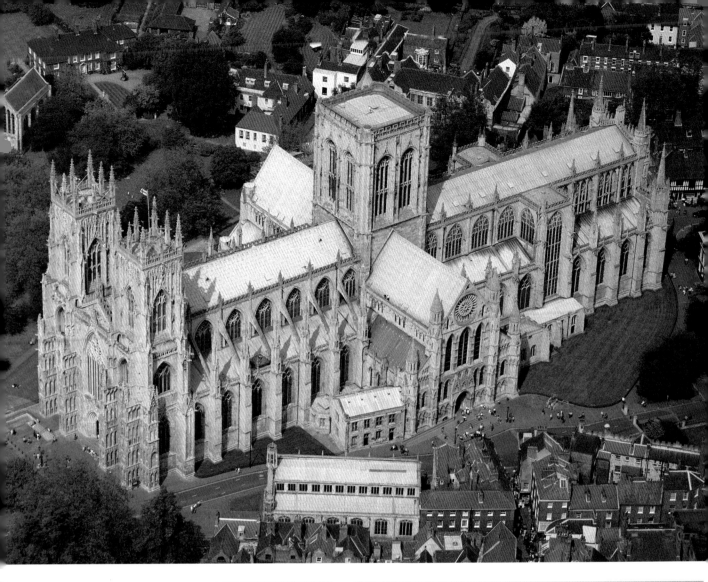

YORK MINSTER *above*

YORK MINSTER IS THE LARGEST GOTHIC church in England and, along with Canterbury, is the seat of an Archbishop. The first Christian Caesar, Constantine, was proclaimed in York and there is a statue of him outside the church today. York became the centre of Christian missionary work during the Anglo-Saxon period and several churches are known to have existed on the site.

The present Minster was built between the 12th and the 15th centuries and is 524ft (159.57m) long and 249ft (79m) wide. The lantern tower is 234ft (71m) high.

York was not seriously affected by the dissolution of the monasteries and even emerged from the Civil War relatively unscathed, when Sir Thomas Fairfax personally ordered its preservation. York is thus one of the few cathedrals with intact medieval stained-glass windows. Unfortunately fires in the early 19th century destroyed the medieval choir stalls and a fire in 1984 extensively damaged the wooden roof.

✳

RIPON *left*

RIPON CATHEDRAL STANDS ON THE SITE of one of England's earliest stone churches. Only the crypt of the church built by St Wilfrid in 607 now survives. The present building is the third on the site and was begun in the 12th century. The Early English west front was completed in 1220, its twin towers originally finished with wooden spires. Significant restoration and alterations took place after 1485 when the nave was widened and the central tower rebuilt. The elaborately carved misericords also date from this period. Further work was halted when the monasteries were dissolved and the churches' revenues were appropriated by the Crown.

DURHAM CATHEDRAL BEGAN LIFE as a shrine for St Cuthbert. The present building was started in 1093 and substantially completed by 1133. It has changed little since and presents a fine example of Romanesque and early Gothic architecture. The nave is dominated by massive, strikingly decorated cylindrical columns and surmounted by an elegant rib vaulted ceiling.

The cathedral still houses the tomb of St Cuthbert as well as the bones of the Venerable Bede, which were placed there in 1370. The 14th-century Caen stone altar screen originally contained 107 alabaster figures but many were vandalised at the end of the 16th century. Further damage was caused in 1650 when 4,000 Scots prisoners were held in the cathedral by Cromwell. Restoration work to the cathedral has been sensitively carried out since that period.

LLANDAFF *above*

LLANDAFF CATHEDRAL WAS BUILT ON the site of a 6th-century religious community founded by St Teilo. It continues to house his shrine. The present cathedral was begun in 1120 but only a Norman arch and traces of some windows remain from that period. Most of Llandaff was completed in 1250 but improvements continued until the 14th century. Uniquely among British cathedrals the building has neither transepts nor a triforium.

The cathedral suffered greatly during the Civil War when the nave was used as a tavern and post office and the font as a pig and horse trough. The cathedral also lost its library and many of its statues and other decorations at this time. Restoration was carried out in 1882 but a German landmine caused major damage in 1941. The cathedral has now been restored once again and features Jacob Epstein's sculpture *Majestas* along with its surviving medieval treasures.

ST DAVID'S *right*

ST DAVID'S CATHEDRAL WAS AN IMPORTANT place of pilgrimage during the middle ages; two pilgrimages to the shrine of the patron saint of Wales were the spiritual equivalent of one pilgrimage to Rome. A monastery was founded on the site in the 6th century but the present building dates from 1176. It was constructed in local Cambrian sandstone in the Norman Transitional style.

The original tower collapsed due to inadequate foundations in the early 13th century and further damage was caused by an earthquake. Major remodelling took place in the 14th century. The nave is made up of alternating round and octagonal piers but has required much additional support in the form of external props, flying buttresses and a suspended ceiling.

In the 19th century Sir George Gilbert Scott provided new foundations and rebuilt the tower. He also recreated the 15th-century roof using authentic medieval methods and materials.

EDINBURGH ST MARY'S EPISCOPALIAN *above*

WHEN THE REFORMED CHURCH in Scotland split over the issue of the Stuart succession in 1689 the loyalist Episcopal Church was deprived of its cathedral. An old woollen mill was used for services until the middle of the 19th century when a generous bequest provided funds for a new church. This was designed by Sir George Gilbert Scott and work began in 1874. The building was opened in 1879 and the congregation was able to move out of a temporary iron church that stood on the site of the present Song School.

The Gothic-style cathedral features unique internal diagonal buttresses which support the 270ft (82m) main spire. The stress is carried through the walls and stabilised by four solid stone pinnacles on the outside of the building. Two further spires make the cathedral an instantly recognisable part of the Edinburgh skyline.

EDINBURGH ST GILES *below*

THE OLDEST PARTS OF ST GILES, in the form of four massive central pillars, date from about 1120. As with most medieval cathedrals it was constantly repaired and remodelled so that by the middle of the 16th century there were around 50 altars in the church. The cathedral was a centre of controversy during the Reformation. John Knox became minister of St Giles in 1559 and developed much of the Scottish form of worship there. In the 1630s bishops were imposed by Charles I, leading to riots, the signing of the National Covenant, and eventually Civil War.

Under Knox St Giles was split into many rooms and used for a variety of purposes. Parts of St Giles have thus been a police station, a fire station, a school, a prison and a coal store as well as the meeting places for the General Assembly of the Church of Scotland, Parliament and Edinburgh City Council.

✳

GLASGOW ST MUNGO *below*

THE TOMB OF ST MUNGO, AN EARLY Christian missionary who died in 603, is in the Lower Church of the Cathedral which bears his name. Many churches have stood on the site but the present building, the oldest in Glasgow, dates from 1197. The nave was extended and completed in the early 13th century, while the Choir and the Lower Church were added some years later. The whole church may have been completed before the end of the 13th century.

After the Reformation the church was divided in two by a wall across the nave. The western section was used by a congregation known as the Outer High, while the Lower Church was used by the Barony. A third congregation, sometimes known as the Inner High, worshipped in the Choir. The Lower Church was for a time filled with soil and used as a burial ground for members of the Barony. Work began on restoring the cathedral to its present state in the early 19th century.

DUNDEE ST PAUL'S *above*

IN THE MID-19TH CENTURY the city of Dundee was highly prosperous, thanks to the jute industry, but had no permanent Episcopalian church. The situation changed when the new Bishop of Brechin decided to make Dundee his permanent residence in 1847. The cathedral of St Paul was begun in 1853 and completed two years later in 1855 at a cost of more than £14,000. It was designed by Sir George Gilbert Scott in the Decorated Gothic style and is dominated by a 210ft (64m) high spire. St Paul's was raised to Cathedral status in 1905.

St Andrews *above*

FOUNDED IN 1160, ST ANDREWS CATHEDRAL was the largest edifice ever built in Scotland until modern times. It was originally 320ft (97.5m) long and 168ft (51m) across its transepts but it was later extended to over 391ft (119m). Major building works (and occasional setbacks caused by storm and fire) continued until 1318 when the cathedral was finally consecrated in the presence of King Robert the Bruce. As the repository of the relics of the apostle St Andrew the cathedral was immensely popular as a centre of pilgrimage in the middle ages.

During the Reformation St Andrews was at the centre of religious controversy. Many martyrs were burnt at the stake within sight of the cathedral. However, the forces of reform were eventually victorious and the cathedral suffered badly at their hands. After a three-day sermon by John Knox a mob sacked and looted the cathedral. Worship at the cathedral came to an end and its stones were used in other local buildings.

First published in 2010 by Myriad Books Limited
35 Bishopsthorpe Road, London SE26 4PA

www. myriadbooks.com

Text copyright © John Mannion

John Mannion has asserted his right under the Copyright, Designs and Patents Act 1998 to be identified as the author of this work.

ISBN 1 84746 342 8
EAN 978 1 84746 342 5

Designed by Jerry Goldie Graphic Design
Printed in China

All of the photographs in this book have been supplied by Skyscan Photolibrary. Skyscan have been involved in aerial photography since 1984, taking and organising new photographic projects as well as running a photolibrary of stock aerial images. They represent the work of many aerial and aviation photographers worldwide as well as their own Skyscan ™ Balloon Camera collection of British towns and landscapes. Further information can be found on their website www.Skyscan.co.uk

All photographs are copyright Skyscan apart from the following which were captured by associates and contributing photographers to the Skyscan Photolibrary: 2,3,4,5,8 (top),15 (top),19, 20 (bottom), 21, Flight Images; 6, 8 (bottom), back cover, E Clack; 11 (top), B Evans; 12, Jarrold Publishing; 13, A Sanger-Davies; 15 (bottom), B Croxford; 17, 24 (bottom), W Cross; 22, Realistic; 24 (top), APS (UK); 25, A Hunter; 26, M Bradbury; 28, 29, 30, K Whitcombe; 31, P Boardman; 32, R West.